Born in 1982

by

Kerry Butters.

Born in 1982

Millennium: **2nd millennium**

Centuries: 19th century – **20th century** – 21st century

Decades: 1950s 1960s 1970s – **1980s** – 1990s 2000s 2010s

Years: 1979 1980 1981 – **1982** – 1983 1984 1985

1982 (MCMLXXXII) was a common year starting on Friday (dominical letter C) of the Gregorian calendar, the 1982nd year of the Common Era (CE) and *Anno Domini* (AD) designations, the 982nd year of the 2nd millennium, the 82nd year of the 20th century, and the 3rd year of the 1980s decade.

Contents

- 1 Events
- 2 Births
- 3 Deaths
- 4 Nobel Prizes
- 5 In the News

Events

January

- January 1 – New ITV franchises, Central, TVS and TSW, are launched.
- January 7 – The Commodore 64 8-bit home computer is launched by Commodore International in Las Vegas (released in August); it becomes the all-time best-selling single personal computer model.
- January 8 – AT&T Corporation agrees to break up and divest itself of 22 subdivisions.
- January 11 – Mark Thatcher, son of British Prime Minister Margaret Thatcher, disappears in the Sahara during the Dakar Rally; he is rescued January 14.
- January 11 – January 17 – A brutal cold snap sends temperatures to all-time record lows in dozens of cities throughout the Midwestern United States.
- January 13 – Shortly after takeoff, Air Florida Flight 90 crashes into Washington, D.C.'s 14th Street Bridge and falls into the Potomac River, killing 78. On the same day, a Washington Metro train derails to the north, killing 3 (the system's first fatal accident).
- January 17 – Cold Sunday sweeps over the northern United States.
- January 18 – 1982 Thunderbirds Indian Springs Diamond Crash: Four Northrop T-38 aircraft of the United States Air Force Thunderbirds Demonstration Squadron crash at Indian Springs Air Force Auxiliary Field, Nevada, killing all 4 pilots.
- January 26
  - Mauno Koivisto is elected President of Finland.

- ○ Unemployment in the United Kingdom increases by 129,918 to 3,070,621, a post-war record number.
- January 27 – The Garret FitzGerald government of the Republic of Ireland is defeated 82–81 on its budget; the 22nd Dáil Éireann is dissolved.
- January 28 – United States Army Brigadier General James L. Dozier is rescued by the Italian anti-terrorism Nucleo Operativo Centrale di Sicurezza (NOCS) force after being held captive for 42 days by the Red Brigades.
- January 30 – The first computer virus, the Elk Cloner, written by 15-year old Rich Skrenta, is found. It infects Apple II computers via floppy disk.

February

- February 1 – Senegal and Gambia form a loose Senegambia Confederation.
- February 2 – The Hama massacre begins in Syria.
- February 3 – Syrian president Hafez al-Assad orders the army to purge the city of Harran of the Muslim Brotherhood.
- February 5 – London-based Laker Airways collapses, leaving 6,000 stranded passengers and debts of $270 million.
- February 7 – Iraqi club Al-Shorta win the 1982 Arab Club Champions Cup with a 4–2 aggregate win over Al-Nejmeh in the final.
- February 9 – Japan Airlines Flight 350 crashes in Tokyo Bay due to thrust reversal on approach to Tokyo International Airport, killing 24 among the 174 people on board.
- February 15 – The oil platform *Ocean Ranger* sinks during a storm off the coast of Newfoundland, killing all 84 rig workers aboard.
- February 18 – The Republic of Ireland general election gives a boost to Fianna Fáil.
- February 19 – The DeLorean Motor Company Car Factory in Belfast is put into receivership.
- February 24 – In South Africa, 22 National Party MPs led by Andries Treurnicht vote for no confidence in P. W. Botha.

- February 25 – The European Court of Human Rights rules that teachers who cane, belt or tase children against the wishes of their parents are in breach of the Human Rights Convention.
- February 27 – Atlanta murders of 1979–81: Wayne Williams is convicted of murdering 2 adult men and is sentenced to two consecutive life terms.

March

- March 3 – Elizabeth II opens the Barbican Centre in London.
- March 9 – Charles Haughey becomes Taoiseach of the Republic of Ireland.
- March 10
  - The United States places an embargo on Libyan oil imports, alleging Libyan support for terrorist groups.
  - Syzygy: All 8 planets align on the same side of the Sun (see also *The Jupiter Effect*).
- March 16 – In Newport, Rhode Island, Claus von Bülow is found guilty of the attempted murder of his wife.
- March 18
  - An Argentine scrap metal dealer raises the Argentine flag in South Georgia.
  - Mary Whitehouse's private prosecution of *The Romans in Britain* collapses.
- March 26 – A ground-breaking ceremony for the Vietnam Veterans Memorial is held in Washington, D.C.
- March 29
  - Royal Assent is given to the Canada Act 1982, setting the stage for the repatriation of the Canadian Constitution on April 17.
  - The 54th Academy Awards, hosted by Johnny Carson, are held at the Dorothy Chandler Pavilion in Los Angeles. *Chariots of Fire* wins Best Picture and 3 other Academy Awards.

April

- April 2 – The Falklands War begins: Argentina invades and occupies the Falkland Islands.
- April 4 – Mexico's children's festival "Juguemos a Cantar" takes place and ends its first run on May 2 .
- April 6 – A blizzard unprecedented in size for April dumps 1–2 feet of snow on the northeastern United States, closing schools and businesses, snarling traffic, and canceling several major league baseball games.
- April 17 – By Proclamation of the Queen of Canada on Parliament Hill, Canada patriates its constitution, gaining full political independence from the United Kingdom; included is the country's first entrenched bill of rights.
- April 23 – Dennis Wardlow, mayor of Key West, Florida, declares the independent "Conch Republic" for a day.
- April 24 – German singer Nicole wins the Eurovision Song Contest 1982 for Germany, with the song "Ein Bisschen Frieden".
- April 25 – Israel completes its withdrawal from the Sinai Peninsula in accordance with the Egypt–Israel Peace Treaty of 1979.
- April 26 – Falklands War: British troops retake South Georgia during Operation Paraquet.
- April 30 – The Bijon Setu massacre takes place in India.

May

- May 1 – A crowd of over 100,000 attends the first day of the 1982 World's Fair in Knoxville, Tennessee, which is kicked off with an address by President Ronald Reagan. Over 11 million people attend during its 6-month run.
- May 2
  - Falklands War: The nuclear submarine HMS *Conqueror* sinks the Argentine cruiser *General Belgrano*, killing 323 sailors. Operation Algeciras, an attempt to destroy a Royal Navy warship in Gibraltar, fails.
  - The Weather Channel airs on cable television for the first time.

- May 4 – Falklands War: HMS *Sheffield* is hit by an Exocet missile, and burns out of control; 20 sailors are killed. The ship sinks on May 10.
- May 5 – A Unabomber bomb explodes in the computer science department at Vanderbilt University; secretary Janet Smith is injured.
- May 8 – French-Canadian racing driver Gilles Villeneuve is killed during qualifying for the Belgian Grand Prix.
- May 12
  - Spanish priest Juan María Fernández y Krohn tries to stab Pope John Paul II with a bayonet during the latter's pilgrimage to the shrine at Fátima.
  - Braniff International Airways is declared bankrupt and ceases all flights.
- May 16 – The New York Islanders sweep the Vancouver Canucks in 4 games to win the 1982 Stanley Cup Final.
- May 18 – Falklands War: The British Special Air Service launches an operation to destroy three Argentinean Exocet missiles and five Super Étendard fighter-bombers in mainland Argentina. It fails when the Argentineans discover about the plot.
- May 21 – Falklands War: British landings spark the Battle of San Carlos.
- May 22
  - Falklands War: HMS *Ardent* is sunk by Argentine aircraft, killing 22 sailors.
  - The International Maritime Organization (IMO) is established.
- May 23 – Falklands War: HMS *Antelope* is lost.
- May 24
  - Iranian troops retake Khorramshahr.
  - KGB head Yuri Andropov is appointed to the Secretariat of the Communist Party of the Soviet Union.
- May 25 – British ships HMS *Coventry* and SS *Atlantic Conveyor* are sunk during the Falklands War; Coventry by two A-4C Skyhawks and the latter sunk by an Exocet.
-

- May 26
  - Aston Villa wins the European Cup, beating Bayern Munich 1–0 after a 69-minute goal by Peter Withe in Rotterdam.
  - Kielder Water, an artificial lake in Northumberland, is opened.
- May 27
  - Tottenham Hotspur F.C. wins the FA Cup, beating Queens Park Rangers 1–0 in a replay.
  - Conservative candidate Tim Smith holds the seat of Beaconsfield in a by-election. The Labour Party candidate is future Prime Minister Tony Blair.
- May 28 – Pope John Paul II's visit to the United Kingdom, the first by a reigning pope, begins.
- May 28 – 29 – Falklands War: Battle of Goose Green: British forces defeat a larger Argentine force.
- May 30
  - Spain becomes the 16th member of NATO and the first nation to enter the alliance since West Germany's admission in 1955.
  - Indianapolis 500: In what Indianapolis Motor Speedway historian Donald Davidson and Speedway public address announcer Tom Carnegie later call the greatest moment in the track's history, 1973 winner Gordon Johncock wins his second race over 1979 winner Rick Mears by 0.16 seconds. Leading to the closest finish to this date, Mears drew alongside Johncock with a lap remaining, after erasing a seemingly insurmountable advantage of more than 11 seconds in the final 10 laps.
  - Hussain Muhammad Ershad seizes power in Bangladesh.
  - Cal Ripken, Jr. plays the first of what eventually becomes his record-breaking streak of 2,632 consecutive Major League Baseball games.

June

- June 6
  - The 1982 Lebanon War begins: Forces under Israeli Defense Minister Ariel Sharon invade southern Lebanon in their "Operation Peace for the Galilee," eventually reaching as far north as the capital Beirut.
  - The United Nations Security Council votes to demand that Israel withdraw its troops from Lebanon.
- June 8
  - President Ronald Reagan becomes the first American chief executive to address a joint session of the British Parliament.
  - Falklands War: British ship RFA *Sir Galahad* is destroyed during the Bluff Cove Air Attacks
  - VASP Flight 168, a Boeing 727 passenger jet, crashes into forest Fortaleza, killing 137.
- June 11
  - U.S. release date of *E.T.: The Extra-Terrestrial*, which would become the biggest box-office hit for the rest of the decade (and beyond).
- June 12 – The Nuclear Disarmament Rally, an event against nuclear weapon proliferation, draws 750,000 to New York City's Central Park. Jackson Browne, James Taylor, Bruce Springsteen, and Linda Ronstadt attend. An international convocation at The Cathedral of St. John the Divine features prominent peace activists from around the world and afterward participants march on Fifth Avenue to Central Park for the rally.
- June 13
  - The 1982 FIFA World Cup begins in Spain.
  - Fahd becomes King of Saudi Arabia upon the death of his brother, Khalid.
- June 14 – The Falklands War ends: Formal surrender of Argentine forces, and liberation of the Falkland Islanders.
- June 18 – Argentine military dictator Leopoldo Galtieri resigns, in the wake of his country's defeat in the Falklands War.

- June 19 – The body of "God's Banker", Roberto Calvi, chairman of Banco Ambrosiano, is found hanging beneath Blackfriars Bridge in London.
- June 21 – Prince William is born at St Mary's Hospital in Paddington, West London.
- June 24 – British Airways Flight 9 suffers a temporary four-engine flameout and damage to the exterior of the plane, after flying through the otherwise undetected ash plume from Indonesia's Mount Galunggung.
- June 25 – The Institute for Puerto Rican Policy is founded in New York City to research and advocate for Puerto Rican and Latino community issues. In 2006, it changes its name to the National Institute for Latino Policy.
- June 30 – The Equal Rights Amendment falls short of the 38 states needed to pass; Phyllis Schlafly and other leaders of the Christian right take credit for its defeat.

July

- July 2
  - Larry Walters, a.k.a. Lawn Chair Larry, flies 16,000 feet (4,900 m) above Long Beach, California, in a lawn chair with weather balloons attached.
  - Roy Jenkins is elected Leader of the Social Democratic Party.
- July 3 – ASLEF train drivers in the United Kingdom go on strike over hours of work; they return to work on July 18.
- July 4 – Four Iranian diplomats are kidnapped upon Israel's invasion of Lebanon.
- July 6 – A lunar eclipse (umbral duration 236 min and total duration 106 min, the longest of the 20th century) occurs.
- July 9
  - Pan Am Flight 759 (Boeing 727) crashes in Kenner, Louisiana, killing all 146 on board and 8 on the ground.
  - Intruder Michael Fagan breaches Buckingham Palace security as far as into the bedroom of Elizabeth II.

- July 11 – Italy beats West Germany 3–1 to win the 1982 FIFA World Cup in Spain.
- July 12 – Checker Motors Corporation ceases production of automobiles.
- July 15 – Geoffrey Prime, a GCHQ civil servant, is remanded in custody on charges under the Official Secrets Act 1911.
- July 16 – In New York City, the Reverend Sun Myung Moon is sentenced to 18 months in prison and fined $25,000 for tax fraud and conspiracy to obstruct justice.
- July 19 – William Whitelaw, Home Secretary, announces that Michael Trestrail (the Queen's bodyguard) has resigned from the Metropolitan Police Service over a relationship with a male prostitute.
- July 20 – The Provisional IRA detonates 2 bombs in central London, killing 8 soldiers, wounding 47 people, and leading to the deaths of 7 horses.
- July 21 – HMS *Hermes*, the Royal Navy flagship during the Falklands War, returns home to Portsmouth to a hero's welcome.
- July 23
  - The International Whaling Commission decides to end commercial whaling by 1985–1986.
  - A coroner's jury returns a verdict of suicide on Roberto Calvi, who was found hanging under Blackfriars Bridge.
  - Torrential rain and mudslides in Nagasaki, Japan destroy bridges and kill 299.
  - On a movie set, the *Twilight Zone* actor Vic Morrow and 2 child actors die in a helicopter stunt accident.
- July 31 – In Beaune, France, 53 persons, 46 of them children, die in a highway accident (France's worst).

August

- August 1 – Attempted coup against government of Daniel Arap Moi in Kenya.
- August 3 – Venezuela recognizes the Sahrawi Arab Democratic Republic (SADR).

- August 4 – The United Nations Security Council votes to censure Israel because its troops are still in Lebanon.
- August 7 – Italian Prime Minister Giovanni Spadolini resigns.
- August 11 – Suriname recognizes the Sahrawi Arab Democratic Republic (SADR).
- August 12 – Mexico announces it is unable to pay its large foreign debt, triggering a debt crisis that quickly spreads throughout Latin America.
- August 13 – In Hong Kong, health warnings on cigarette packets are made statutory.
- August 17 – The first compact discs (CDs) are released to the public in Germany.
- August 20 – Lebanese Civil War: A multinational force lands in Beirut to oversee the PLO withdrawal from Lebanon. French troops arrive August 21, U.S. Marines August 25.

September

- September 3 – Italian general Carlo Alberto Dalla Chiesa is killed in a Mafia ambush.
- September 5 – Iowa paperboy Johnny Gosch is kidnapped.
- September 14 – Lebanese President-elect Bachir Gemayel is assassinated in Beirut.
- September 18 – A Lebanese Christian militia (the Phalange) kill thousands of Palestinians in the Sabra and Shatila refugee camps in West Beirut, the massacre is a response to the assassination of president-elect, Bachir Gemayel four days earlier.
- September 19 – The first emoticons are posted by Scott Fahlman.
- September 21
  - The first International Day of Peace is proclaimed by the (United Nations).
  - The National Football League Players Association calls a strike, the first in-season work stoppage in the National Football League's 63-year history. The strike lasts for 57 days, reduces the regular season from 16 games to 9, and forces an expanded 16-team playoff tournament.

- September 23 – Amine Gemayel, brother of Bachir, is elected president of Lebanon.
- September 24 – The Wimpy Operation, first act of armed resistance against Israeli troops in Beirut.
- September 25 – In Israel, 400,000 marchers demand the resignation of Prime Minister Menachem Begin.
- September 26 – Thermals take Australian parachutist Rich Collins up to 2,800 metres (9,200 ft) during a jump; he almost blacks out due to lack of oxygen. He releases his main parachute to fall to lower altitude and lands by his reserve parachute.
- September 29 – October 1 – The Chicago Tylenol murders occur when 7 people in the Chicago area die after ingesting capsules laced with potassium cyanide.

October

- October 1
  - Helmut Kohl replaces Helmut Schmidt as Chancellor of Germany through a constructive vote of no confidence.
  - In Orlando, Florida, Walt Disney World opens the second largest theme park, EPCOT Center, to the public for the first time.
  - Sony launches the first consumer compact disc (CD) player (model CDP-101).
- October 4
  - Glenn Gould, Canadian pianist, dies from a stroke. Later, his recently re-recorded "Aria" from the Goldberg Variations, by J.S. Bach, is played at the end of his funeral service.
- October 8
  - Poland bans Solidarity after having suspended it on 13 December 1981.
  - After six years in opposition, Social Democrat Olof Palme becomes once again Prime Minister of Sweden .
- October 11 – The *Mary Rose*, flagship of Henry VIII of England that sank in 1545, is raised from the Solent.

- October 12 – Thorbjörn Fälldin returns as Prime Minister of Sweden .
- October 13 – The Ford Sierra is launched in Europe, replacing the Ford Cortina (which was known as the Ford Taunus on continental Europe).
- October 19 – John DeLorean is arrested for selling cocaine to undercover FBI agents (he is later found not guilty due to entrapment).
- October 20
  - Luzhniki disaster: During the UEFA Cup match between FC Spartak Moscow and HFC Haarlem, 66 people are crushed to death.
- October 27
  - In Canada, Dominion Day is officially renamed Canada Day.
  - The Homosexual Offences (Northern Ireland) Order 1982 comes into effect, decriminalising homosexuality in Northern Ireland for those aged 18 or older.
- October 28 – The Socialist Party wins the election in Spain; Felipe González is elected Prime Minister.

November

- November 2 – Channel 4, a British public-service television broadcaster, is launched, with Richard Whiteley's *Countdown* being the first program to be broadcast.
- November 3
  - A gasoline or petrol tanker explodes in the Salang Tunnel in Afghanistan, killing at least 176 people.
  - The Dow Jones Industrial Average surges 43.41 points, or 4.25%, to close at 1,065.49, its first all-time high in more than 9 years. It last hit a record on January 11, 1973 when the average closed at 1,051.70. The points gain is the biggest ever up to this point.
- November 6 – Cameroon president Ahmadou Ahidjo resigns, replaced by Paul Biya.
- November 7 – The Thames Barrier is first publicly demonstrated.

- November 8 – Kenan Evren becomes the seventh president of Turkey as a result of constitution referendum. His former title was **head of state**.
- November 12 – In the Soviet Union, former KGB head Yuri Andropov is selected to become the general secretary of the Soviet Communist Party's Central Committee, succeeding the late Leonid I. Brezhnev.
- November 13 – The Vietnam Veterans Memorial is dedicated in Washington, D.C., after a march to its site by thousands of Vietnam War veterans.
- November 14 – The leader of Poland's outlawed Solidarity movement, Lech Wałęsa, is released from 11 months of internment near the Soviet border.
- November 20
  - The General Union of Ecuadorian Workers (UGTE) is founded.
  - University of California, Berkeley executes "The Play" in a college football game against Stanford. Completing a wacky 57-yard kickoff return that includes five laterals, Kevin Moen runs through Stanford band members who had prematurely come onto the field. His touchdown stands and California wins 25–20.
- November 25 – The Minneapolis Thanksgiving Day fire destroys an entire city block of downtown Minneapolis, including the headquarters of Northwestern National Bank.
- November 27 – Yasuhiro Nakasone becomes Prime Minister of Japan.
- November 28
  - Representatives from 88 countries gather in Geneva to discuss world trade and ways to work toward aspects of free trade.
  - The Edmonton Eskimos win an unprecedented 5th consecutive Grey Cup; a feat yet unaccomplished by any professional football franchise to win the 70th Grey Cup defeating the Toronto Argonauts 32-16.

- November 30 – Michael Jackson releases *Thriller*, the biggest selling album of all time.

December

- December 1 – Miguel de la Madrid takes office as President of Mexico.
- December 2 – At the University of Utah, 61-year-old retired dentist Barney Clark becomes the first person to receive a permanent artificial heart (he lives for 112 days with the device).
- December 3 – A final soil sample is taken from the site of Times Beach, Missouri. It is found to contain 300 times the safe level of dioxin.
- December 4 – The People's Republic of China adopts its current constitution.
- December 7 – The first U.S. execution by lethal injection is carried out in Texas.
- December 8 – The December murders occur in Suriname.
- December 11 – Pop group ABBA make their final public performance on the British TV programme *The Late, Late Breakfast Show*.
- December 12 – Women's peace protest at RAF Greenham Common: 30,000 women hold hands and form a human chain around the 14.5 km (9 mi) perimeter fence.
- December 13 – The 6.0 Ms North Yemen earthquake shakes southwestern Yemen with a maximum Mercalli intensity of VIII (*Severe*), killing 2,800.
- December 14 – Bolivia recognizes the Sahrawi Arab Democratic Republic (SADR).
- December 16 – The United Freedom Front bombs an office of South African Airways in Elmont, NY and an IBM office in Harrison, NY. Two police officers suffer hearing damage. The UFF claimed responsibility for the IBM building bombing in March 1984, stating that the company was targeted because of its business in South Africa under Apartheid.

- December 22 – The Indian Ocean Commission (Commission de l'Océan Indien) (COI) is created by Port Louis Agreement.
- December 23 – The United States Environmental Protection Agency recommends the evacuation of Times Beach, Missouri due to dangerous levels of dioxin contamination.
- December 24 – The "Christmas Eve Blizzard of '82" hits Denver.
- December 26 – *Time* magazine's Man of the Year is given for the first time to a non-human, the computer.
- December 29 – Paul "Bear" Bryant coaches his final college football game, leading Alabama to a 21-15 victory over Illinois in the Liberty Bowl at Memphis. Bryant died of a massive heart attack four weeks later at age 69.

Date unknown

- The population of the People's Republic of China alone exceeds 1 billion making China the first nation to have a population of more than 1 billion.
- A global surplus of crude oil causes gasoline prices to collapse.
- A brief but severe recession begins in the United States.
- Seattle is officially dubbed the *Emerald City* after a contest is held to choose a new city slogan.
- George Stigler is awarded Nobel Memorial Prize in Economic Sciences.
- The car brand Toyota Camry is introduced.
- Jonathan Schell's *The Fate of the Earth*, published in book format in the United States, warns of the dangers of the nuclear arms race.
- Dorling Kindersley, formerly a book packager, begins publishing.
- In a Gallup poll, 51% of Americans do not accept homosexuality as normal.
- The first China Central Television New Year's Gala program starts. This program is watched by 1.1 billion Chinese every year.

Births

January

Eddie Redmayne

Catherine, Duchess of Cambridge

Dwyane Wade

Adam Lambert

Jodie Sweetin

- January 1 – David Nalbandian, Argentine tennis player
- January 2 – Kevin Dudley, American football player
- January 3 – Chisu, Finnish singer-songwriter
- January 4
  - Kang Hye-jung, South Korean actress
  - Richard Logan, English footballer
- January 5
  - Janica Kostelić, Croatian skier
  - Vadims Vasiļevskis, Latvian javelin thrower
- January 6
  - Eddie Redmayne, English actor
  - Gilbert Arenas, American basketball player
- January 7
  - Francisco Rodríguez, Venezuelan baseball player
  - Camilo Villegas, Colombian golfer
- January 9 – Catherine, Duchess of Cambridge, British princess
-

- January 10
  - Ana Layevska, Ukrainian–born, Mexican singer and actress
  - Misato Fukuen, Japanese voice actress
- January 11 – Ashley Taylor Dawson, English singer and actor
- January 12 – Dontrelle Willis, American baseball player
- January 13
  - Guillermo Coria, Argentine tennis player
  - Ruth Wilson, English actress
- January 14
  - Caleb Followill, American singer
  - Víctor Valdés, Spanish football player
- January 15 – Benjamin Agosto, American skater
- January 17 – Dwyane Wade, American professional basketball player
- January 18
  - Quinn Allman, American guitarist
  - Joanna Newsom, American singer, harpist, pianist and songwriter
- January 19 – Jodie Sweetin, American actress
- January 20 – Erin Wasson, American model and actress
- January 21 – Go Shiozaki, Japanese professional wrestler
- January 22
  - Liane Bahler, German professional cyclist (d. 2007)
  - Jason Peters, American football player
- January 23
  - Patrick Levis, American actor
  - Karol Bielecki, Polish handball player
- January 25
  - Sho Sakurai, Japanese singer
  - Noemi, Italian singer
- January 26 – Brahim Takioullah, Moroccan *Guinness World Records*-holder for largest feet
- January 28 – Ainett Stephens, Venezuelan television personality/model
- January 29
  - Adam Lambert, American singer

- ○ Heidi Mueller, American actress
- January 31 – Elena Paparizou, Greek-Swedish singer

February

Alice Eve

Lupe Fiasco

Nate Ruess

- February 1
  - ○ Gavin Henson, Welsh rugby union player
  - ○ Iness Chepkesis Chenonge, Kenyan athlete
  - ○

- February 2
  - Kelly Mazzante, American basketball player
  - Filippo Magnini, Italian swimmer
  - Li-Mei Chiang, Japanese actress
- February 3
  - Vera Brezhneva, Ukrainian and Russian pop-singer and television presenter
  - Jessica Harp, American songwriter and former country artist
- February 4
  - Mandisa Stevenson, American basketball player
  - Tomas Vaitkus, Lithuanian professional road racing cyclist
- February 5
  - Kevin Everett, American football player
  - Yū Kobayashi, Japanese voice actress
- February 6 – Alice Eve, English actress
- February 8 – Zersenay Tadese, Eritrean long distance track/road running athlete
- February 9 – Ami Suzuki, Japanese singer
- February 10
  - Justin Gatlin, American athlete
  - Mon Redee Sut Txi, Malaysian athlete
  - Yoshimasa Hosoya, Japanese voice actor
- February 11
  - Natalie Dormer, English actress
  - Neil Robertson, Australian snooker player
- February 13 – Lanisha Cole, American model
- February 14 – Marián Gáborík, Czechoslovakian (now Slovakia) hockey player
- February 16 – Lupe Fiasco, American rapper
- February 17
  - Daniel Merriweather, Australian singer
  - Adriano Leite Ribeiro, Brazilian footballer
- February 18 – Jessie Ward, American actress
- February 19 – Camelia Potec, Romanian swimmer
- February 22

- o Buğra Gülsoy, Turkish actor, architect, director, graphic designer and photographer
  - o Jenna Haze, American pornographic actress
  - o Kelly Johnson, American baseball player
- February 25
  - o Chris Baird, Northern Irish footballer
  - o Maria Kanellis, American professional wrestler/model
- February 26 – Nate Ruess, American singer-songwriter
- February 28
  - o Andres Nuiamäe, Estonian soldier (d. 2004)
  - o Natalia Vodianova, Russian model, actress and philanthropist

March

Jessica Biel

Nicoleta Onel

Danica Patrick

- March 2
  - Henrik Lundqvist, Swedish hockey goaltender
  - Ben Roethlisberger, American football player
  - Mike Nugent, American football player
  - Kevin Kurányi, German soccer player
- March 3 – Jessica Biel, American actress
- March 4
  - Landon Donovan, American soccer player
  - Yasemin Mori, Turkish musician
- March 5 – Daniel Carter, New Zealand rugby player
- March 6 – Stephen Jordan, English footballer
- March 8
  - Nicoleta Onel, Romanian gymnast
  - Kat Von D, Mexican-American tattoo artist
- March 9 – Paul Ballard, English television presenter
- March 10
  - Kwame Brown, American basketball player
  - Thomas Middleditch, Canadian actor
- March 11 – Thora Birch, American actress
- March 13 – Jamie Cox, Australian cricketer
- March 15
  - Bobby Boswell, American soccer player
  - Wilson Kipsang Kiprotich, Kenyan long-distance runner
- March 18 – Adam Pally, American actor and comedian
- March 19 – Triana Iglesias, Norwegian model/Playboy Cyber Girl
- March 20 – Nick Wheeler, American musician
- March 21 – Maria Elena Camerin, Italian tennis player
- March 23 – Tomasz Kuszczak, Polish football goalkeeper

- March 24 – Kenichirou Ohashi, Japanese voice actor
- March 25
  - Danica Patrick, American race car driver
  - Sean Faris, American actor
  - Jenny Slate, American actress and comedian
- March 26 – Mikel Arteta, Spanish football player
- March 29 – Hideaki Takizawa, Japanese actor and singer
- March 30
  - Jason Dohring, American actor
  - Philippe Mexès, French footballer
  - Javier Garcia Portillo, Spanish footballer

April

Jay Baruchel

Seth Rogen

Kelly Clarkson

Kirsten Dunst

- April 1
    - Andreas Thorkildsen, Norwegian javelin thrower
    - Taran Killam, American actor and comedian
    - Róbert Vittek, Slovakian football player
- April 2
- David Ferrer, Spanish tennis player
- April 3
    - Jared Allen, American football player
    - Cobie Smulders, Canadian actress
    - Kasumi Nakane, Japanese gravure idol
- April 4
    - Justin Cook, American voice actor
- April 5
    - Hayley Atwell, English actress
    - Matt Pickens, American soccer player
- April 6
    - Ilan Hall, Israeli-American chef

- o Bret Harrison, American actor and singer
- o Euclides Varela, Cape Verdean long-distance runner
- April 7
  - o Sonjay Dutt, Indian American professional wrestler
  - o Kelli Young, English singer
- April 9
  - o Jay Baruchel, Canadian actor
  - o Olímpio Cipriano, Angolan basketball player
- April 10
  - o Chyler Leigh, American actress
  - o Nadia Meikher, Ukrainian mezzo-soprano singer
- April 12 – Easton Corbin, American country music singer
- April 13 – Nellie McKay, American singer
- April 14 – Larissa França, Brazilian beach volleyball player
- April 15 – Seth Rogen, Canadian actor/comedian
- April 18
  - o Scott Hartnell, Canadian hockey player
  - o Marie-Élaine Thibert, Canadian singer
- April 19 – Ignacio Serricchio, Argentine-born American actor
- April 20 – Keiichiro Nagashima, Japanese speed skater
- April 22 – Kaká, Brazilian footballer
- April 24
  - o Kelly Clarkson, American singer
  - o Shayna Nackoney, Canadian synchronized swimmer
- April 25 – Monty Panesar, English cricketer
- April 26
  - o Nadja Benaissa, German pop singer
  - o Jon Lee, English singer and actor
- April 27 – Katrina Johnson, American actress
- April 28
  - o Nikki Grahame, British reality TV star
  - o Donna Feldman, American model and actress
  - o Harry Shum, Jr., Costa Rican dancer and actor.
- April 30
  - o Kirsten Dunst, American actress
  - o Lloyd Banks, American rapper

- ○ Drew Seeley, Canadian actor, singer-songwriter and dancer

May

Jamie Dornan

Rebecca Hall

- May 1
  - ○ Darijo Srna, Croatian soccer player
  - ○ Jamie Dornan, Irish actor
- May 3 – Rebecca Hall, British actress
- May 4
  - ○ Markus Rogan, Austrian swimmer
  - ○ Vera Schmidt, Hungarian singer-songwriter
- May 6 – Jason Witten, American football player
- May 7 – Ákos Buzsáky, Hungarian footballer
- May 8 – Adrian Gonzalez, Mexican-American baseball player
- May 9 – Rachel Boston, American actress
- May 10
  - ○ Adebayo Akinfenwa, English footballer
  - ○ Jeremy Gable, American playwright
- May 11 – Cory Monteith, Canadian actor (d. 2013)

- May 13 – Oguchi Onyewu, American soccer player
- May 14 – Ai Shibata, Japanese swimmer
- May 15
    - Veronica Campbell-Brown, Jamaican athlete
    - Jessica Sutta, American dancer, showgirl, singer
    - Tatsuya Fujiwara, Japanese actor
    - Alexandra Breckenridge, American actress, voice actress, and photographer
- May 17
    - Dylan Macallister, Australian soccer player
    - Tony Parker, French basketball player
- May 19 – Kevin Amankwaah, English footballer
- May 20
    - Petr Čech, Czech footballer
    - Lee Ryol-li, Korean-Japanese boxer
- May 22
    - Apolo Anton Ohno, American short track speed skater and actor
    - Erin McNaught, 2006 Miss Australia
- May 23 – Tristan Prettyman, American singer/songwriter
- May 25 – Alexandr Ivanov, Russian javelin thrower
- May 26 – Yoko Matsugane, Japanese model
- May 27 – Michael de Grussa, Australian musician/comedian
- May 29
    - Ana Beatriz Barros, Brazilian model
    - Anita Briem, Icelandic actress

June

Yelena Isinbayeva

Prince William, Duke of Cambridge

Jarret Stoll

- June 1 – Justine Henin, Belgian tennis player
- June 3 – Yelena Isinbayeva, Russian athlete
- June 5 – Yoo In-na, South Korean actor
- June 7 – Amy Nuttall, British actress and opera singer
- June 8
  - Josh Pence, American actor
  - Nadia Petrova, Russian tennis player
- June 10
  - Tara Lipinski, American figure skater
  - Princess Madeleine of Sweden
- June 11
  - Diana Taurasi, American basketball player
  - Eldar Rønning, Norwegian cross-country skier
- June 12 – Jason David, American football player
- June 13
  - Kenenisa Bekele, Ethiopian long-distance runner
  - Davood Ghadami, English actor
- June 14
  - Jamie Green, English race car driver

- Nicole Irving, Australian swimmer
- Luda Kroitor, Moldavian-born salsa dancer and instructor
- Lang Lang, Chinese pianist
- June 15 – James Lamont, English television writer
- June 16 – Missy Peregrym, Canadian actress
- June 17 – Arthur Darvill, British actor
- June 18 – Marco Borriello, Italian football player
- June 19
  - Mika Kamita, Japanese singer
  - Hugh Everett III, American physicist
- June 21 – Prince William, Duke of Cambridge, British prince
- June 22
  - Soraia Chaves, Portuguese actress and model
  - Ian Kinsler, American baseball player
- June 23 – Joona Puhakka, Finnish diver
- June 24
  - Natasa Dusev-Janics, Serbian-Hungarian sprint canoer
  - Jarret Stoll, Canadian ice hockey player
- June 25 – Mikhail Youzhny, Russian tennis player
- June 27 – Takeru Shibaki, Japanese actor
- June 29
  - Colin Jost, American actor, writer, and comedian
  - Matthew Mercer, American voice actor, screenwriter and director
- June 30 – Lizzy Caplan, American actress

July

Tuba Büyüküstün

Pendleton Ward

Carl Espen

Priyanka Chopra

Jared Padalecki

Paul Wesley

Anna Paquin

Allison Mack

Yvonne Strahovski

- July 1 – Hilarie Burton, American actress and VJ

- July 3
  - Kanika, Indian actress and singer
  - Steph Jones, American singer-songwriter
- July 4
  - Hannah Harper, American porn actress and director
  - Michael Sorrentino, American model, actor, and author
- July 5
  - Alberto Gilardino, Italian footballer
  - Dave Haywood, American singer
  - Paíto, Mozambican footballer
  - Tuba Büyüküstün, Turkish actress
  - Monica Day, American model and journalist
  - Fabrício de Souza, Brazilian footballer
  - Alexander Dimitrenko, Ukrainian-German boxer
  - Julien Féret, French footballer
  - Kate Gynther, Australian water polo player
  - Philippe Gilbert, Belgian cyclist
  - Dave Haywood, American singer-songwriter and guitarist
  - Javier Paredes, Spanish footballer
  - Szabolcs Perenyi, Romanian-Hungarian footballer
  - Beno Udrih, Slovenian basketball player
- July 6
  - Brandon Jacobs, American football player
  - Bree Robertson, Australian gymnast and actress
  - Misty Upham, American actress (d. 2014)
  - Tay Zonday, American actor and singer
- July 7 – Jan Laštůvka, Czech footballer
- July 8
  - Sophia Bush, American actress
  - Hakim Warrick, American basketball player
  - Pendleton Ward, American animator
- July 9
  - Slaine Kelly, Irish actress
  - Sakon Yamamoto, Japanese racecar driver
- July 10
  - Sebastian Mila, Polish footballer

- o Jeffrey Walker, Australian actor and director
- July 12 – Antonio Cassano, Italian footballer
- July 13
  - o Shin-Soo Choo, Korean baseball player
  - o Yadier Molina, Puerto Rican baseball player
- July 15
  - o Cristian Dănălache, Romanian footballer
  - o Carl Espen, Norwegian singer and songwriter
- July 16 – Steven Hooker, Australian pole vaulter
- July 17 – Natasha Hamilton, English singer
- July 18
  - o Priyanka Chopra, Indian actress and beauty queen
  - o Ryan Cabrera, Colombian-American pop rock musician
- July 19
  - o Jared Padalecki, American actor
  - o Katee Shean, American choreographer, actor, and singer
- July 21
  - o Jason Cram, Australian swimmer
  - o Mao Kobayashi, Japanese actress and journalist
- July 23 – Paul Wesley, American actor
- July 24
  - o Anna Paquin, Canadian-born actress
  - o Elisabeth Moss, American actress
- July 25 – Brad Renfro, American actor (d. 2008)
- July 28 – Michael Rose, English footballer
- July 29 – Allison Mack, German-American actress
- July 30
  - o James Anderson, English cricketer
  - o Yvonne Strahovski, Australian actress
  - o Martin Starr, American actor

August

Orelsan

Sebastian Stan

Joleon Lescott

LeAnn Rimes

Andy Roddick

- August 1 – Orelsan, French rapper
- August 2 – Hélder Postiga, Portuguese footballer
- August 5 – Lolo Jones, American track and field athlete
- August 6
  - Kevin van der Perren, Belgian figure skater
  - Romola Garai, English actress
  - Spice, Jamaican dancehall artist
- August 7
  - Yana Klochkova, Ukrainian swimmer
  - Marco Melandri, Italian motorcycle racer
- August 9 – Tyson Gay, American athlete
- August 10
  - Devon Aoki, American supermodel and actress
  - Shaun Murphy, English snooker player
- August 12 – Jon Olsson, Swedish freestyle skier
- August 13
  - Shani Davis, American speed skater
  - Gary McSheffrey, English footballer
  - Sebastian Stan, Romanian-American actor
- August 14 – Larissa França, Brazilian beach volleyball player
- August 15 – Tsuyoshi Hayashi, Japanese actor
- August 16
  - Joleon Lescott, English footballer
  - Todd Haberkorn, American voice actor
- August 17
  - Jon Olsson, Swedish freestyle skier

- o Mark Salling, American actor
- August 19 – Willy Denzey, French singer
- August 20 – Jamil Walker Smith, American actor
- August 21
  - o Akane Omae, Japanese voice actress
  - o Omar Sachedina, Canadian journalist and news anchor
- August 23 – Natalie Coughlin, American Olympic swimmer
- August 24
  - o Kim Källström, Swedish footballer
  - o Jennifer Widerstrom, American personal trainer
- August 26 – John Mulaney, American actor and comedian
- August 28
  - o LeAnn Rimes, American country singer
  - o Karo Parisyan, Armenian MMA fighter
- August 29
  - o Carlos Delfino, Argentine basketball player
  - o Vincent Enyeama, Nigerian football goalkeeper
  - o Leon Washington, American football player
- August 30 – Andy Roddick, American tennis player
- August 31 – José Manuel Reina Páez, Spanish footballer

September

Lil Wayne

Lacey Chabert

Ranbir Kapoor

- September 1 – Jeffrey Buttle, Canadian figure skater
- September 2
    - Alan Tate, British professional footballer
    - Mandy Cho, Hong Kong actress
- September 3
    - Sarah Burke, Canadian freestyle skier (d. 2012)
    - Ayumi Fujimura, Japanese voice actress
- September 5 – Cyndi Wang, Taiwanese singer and actress
- September 7 – Ryōko Shiraishi, Japanese voice actress
- September 9 – Ai Otsuka, Japanese singer, songwriter, pianist and actress
- September 11 – Shriya Saran, Indian actress
- September 12 – Nana Ozaki, Japanese gravure idol
- September 13
    - Nenê, Brazilian basketball player
    - J.G. Quintel, American animator
- September 18 – Lukas Reimann, Swiss politician
- September 19 – Nicole Voss, American model

- September 20 – JJ Jia, Chinese actress
- September 22
  - Kosuke Kitajima, Japanese swimmer
  - Billie Piper, English actress and singer
- September 25 – Hyun Bin, Korean actor
- September 26 – Betty Sun, Chinese actress
- September 27
  - Darrent Williams, American football player (d. 2007)
  - Lil Wayne, African-American rapper
  - Jon McLaughlin, American pop rock singer-songwriter and pianist
  - Ella Scott Lynch, Australian actress
- September 28
  - St. Vincent, American singer, songwriter and multi-instrumentalist
  - Emeka Okafor, American basketball player
  - Megumi Kagurazaka, Japanese actress
  - Abhinav Bindra, Indian shooter
  - Ranbir Kapoor, Indian actor
  - Anderson Varejão, American basketball player
- September 29
  - Ariana Jollee, American porn actress and director
  - Amy Williams, British Olympic medallist
- September 30
  - Lacey Chabert, American actress
  - Kieran Culkin, American actor
  - Michelle Marsh, British model
  - Li Xiaolu, Chinese actress

October

Erik von Detten

Ian Thorpe

Imran Abbas Naqvi

Svetlana Loboda

Matt Smith

- October 1 – Sandra Oxenryd, Swedish pop singer
- October 2 – Tyson Chandler, American basketball player
- October 3 – Erik von Detten, American actor
- October 5 – Zhang Yining, Chinese table tennis player
- October 6
    - MC Lars, American rapper
    - Levon Aronian, Armenian chess Grandmaster
- October 7
    - Madjid Bougherra, Algerian footballer
    - Jermain Defoe, English footballer
    - Robby Ginepri, American tennis player
- October 9 – Travis Rice, American snowboarder
- October 10
    - Jason Oost, Dutch footballer
    - Dan Stevens, British actor
- October 11
    - Salim Stoudamire, American basketball player
    - Valentina Zelyaeva, Russian model
- October 13
    - Ian Thorpe, Australian swimmer
    - Jo Yoon-hee, South Korean actress and model
- October 15
    - Imran Abbas Naqvi, Pakistani actor and model
    - Saif Saaeed Shaheen, Qatarian athlete
    - Jessica Rey, American actress
- October 16 – Svetlana Loboda, Ukrainian singer and composer
- October 17 – Nick Riewoldt, Australian rules footballer
- October 18 or 19 – Shauntay Henderson, American criminal
- October 19 – Louis Oosthuizen, South African golfer
- October 21
    - Matt Dallas, American actor
    - Lee Chong Wei, Malaysian badminton player
- October 22
    - Robinson Canó, Dominican baseball player
    - Heath Miller, American football player
- October 25 – Eman Lam, Hong Kong singer

- October 26 – Nicola Adams, English boxer
- October 27
  - Jessy Matador, Congolese-French singer
  - Dennis Moran, American computer hacker
- October 28
  - Anthony Lerew, American baseball player
  - Matt Smith, English actor
  - Mai Kuraki, Japanese singer
- October 29
  - Ariel Lin, Taiwanese actress and singer
  - Chelan Simmons, Canadian actress

November

Anne Hathaway

Elisha Cuthbert

Ruth Lorenzo

- November 2 – Kyoko Fukada, Japanese actress, model and singer
- November 3 – Pekka Rinne, Finnish ice hockey goaltender
- November 4 – Devin Hester, American Football player
- November 5 – Rob Swire, Australian musician
- November 6 – Sowelu, Japanese singer
- November 8
  - Ted DiBiase, American professional wrestler and actor
  - Ethan Juan, Taiwanese actor
  - Francesco Molinari, Italian golfer
- November 9 – Jana Pittman, Australian athlete
- November 10
  - Ruth Lorenzo, Spanish singer and composer
  - Heather Matarazzo, American actress
- November 11 – Brittny Gastineau, American model and socialite
- November 12
  - Anne Hathaway, American actress
  - Mikele Leigertwood, English footballer
- November 13 – Kumi Koda, Japanese singer
- November 14
  - Sailosi Tagicakibau, Samoan rugby player
  - Joy Williams, American singer/songwriter
- November 15 – Joe Kowalewski, American football player
- November 16 – Amar'e Stoudemire, American professional basketball player
- November 18
  - Akeno Watanabe, Japanese voice actress
  - Damon Wayans, Jr., African-American actor and comedian
- November 19 – Shin Dong-hyuk, North Korean defector and human rights activist

- November 21 – Ioana Ciolacu, Romanian fashion designer
- November 22 – Charlene Choi, Hong Kong singer and actress
- November 23 – Asafa Powell, Jamaican sprinter
- November 25 – Minna Kauppi, Finnish orienteer
- November 26 – Karl Henry, Professional football player
- November 27 – Aleksandr Kerzhakov, Russian soccer player
- November 28 – Steve Mullings, Jamaican athlete
- November 29 – Ashley Force, American race car driver
- November 30
    - Elisha Cuthbert, Canadian actress
    - Clémence Poésy, French actress
    - Jason Pominville, American hockey player

December

Alison Brie

Kristin Kreuk

Anna Sedokova

- December 2
  - Horacio Pancheri, Argentine actor
- December 3
  - Jaycee Chan, Hong Kong actor and singer
  - Michael Essien, Ghanaian footballer
- December 4 – Nick Vujicic, Australian-born director
- December 5 – Keri Hilson, American R&B recording artist, songwriter, and actress
- December 6
  - Ryan Carnes, American actor
  - Alberto Contador, Spanish cyclist
- December 7
  - Chrispa, Greek singer and actress
  - Jack Huston, British actor
- December 8
  - Chrisette Michele, American R&B singer-songwriter
  - Nicki Minaj, Trinidadian-born American rapper, singer, and songwriter
  - Serena Ryder, Canadian musician
- December 9
  - Tamilla Abassova, Russian cyclist
  - Nathalie De Vos, Belgian athlete
  - Ryan Grant, American football player
  - Bastian Swillims, German sprinter
- December 13
  - Anthony Callea, Australian singer
  - Elisa Di Francisca, Italian fencer

- o Ayumi Kinoshita, Japanese model and actress
- December 14 – Anthony Way, British singer and actor
- December 16
  - o Frankie Ballard, American country music singer-songwriter
  - o Mei Finegold, Israeli singer
  - o Stanislav Šesták, Slovakian footballer
  - o Anna Sedokova, Ukrainian singer, actress and television presenter
- December 17 – Onur Özsu, Turkish singer-songwriter
- December 19 – Tero Pitkämäki, Finnish javelin thrower
- December 20
  - o David Wright, American baseball player
  - o David Cook, American singer/songwriter
- December 21 – Mandy Wong, Hong Kong actress
- December 24
  - o Robert Carmine, American singer
  - o Masaki Aiba, Japanese singer
  - o Tetsuya Kakihara, Japanese voice actor
- December 26
  - o Aksel Lund Svindal, Norwegian alpine skier
  - o Shun Oguri, Japanese actor
- December 27 – Terji Skibenæs, Faroese guitarist
- December 29 – Alison Brie, American actress
- December 30 – Kristin Kreuk, Canadian actress
- December 31 – Luke Schenscher, Australian basketball player

Deaths

January

Eduardo Frei Montalva

Stanley Holloway

- January 1 – Victor Buono, American actor (b. 1938)
- January 5
    - Hans Conried, American actor (b. 1917)
    - Harvey Lembeck, American actor (b. 1923)
- January 8 – Reta Shaw, American actress (b. 1912)
- January 10 – Paul Lynde, American actor (b. 1926)
- January 11 – A. W. Haydon, American Invetor(b. 1906)
- January 11 – Jiro Horikoshi, Japanese aircraft designer (b. 1903)
- January 13 – Marcel Camus, French film director (b. 1912)
- January 17 – Juan O'Gorman, Mexican architect (b. 1905)
- January 19 – Elis Regina, Brazilian singer (b. 1945)

- January 22 – Eduardo Frei Montalva, Chilean politician and former President (b. 1904)
- January 26 – Mikhail Suslov, Soviet politician and Politburo member (b. 1902)
- January 30
  - Stanley Holloway, English actor (b. 1890)
  - Lightnin' Hopkins, American musician (b. 1912)

February

- February 4
  - Sue Carol, American actress (b. 1906)
  - Alex Harvey, Scottish musician (b. 1935)
- February 5 – Neil Aggett, South African labor leader (suicide) (b. 1953)
- February 11
  - Eleanor Powell, American dancer (b. 1912)
  - Takashi Shimura, Japanese actor (b. 1905)
- February 12 – Victor Jory, Canadian actor (b. 1902)
- February 17
  - Thelonious Monk, American jazz pianist (b. 1917)
  - Lee Strasberg, American actor and acting coach (b. 1901)
- February 18 – Dame Ngaio Marsh, New Zealand crime fiction writer (b. 1895)
- February 21 – Gershom Scholem, German-born Israeli Jewish philosopher and historian (b. 1897)
- February 24 – Virginia Bruce, American actress (b. 1910)

March

Carl Orff

- March 2 – Philip K. Dick, American author (b. 1928)
- March 5 – John Belushi, American actor (b. 1949)
- March 6 – Ayn Rand, Russian-born author (b. 1905)
- March 8 – Rab Butler, British statesman (b. 1902)
- March 19 – Randy Rhoads, American guitarist for Ozzy Osbourne (b. 1956)
- March 25 – Goodman Ace, American humorist (b. 1899)
- March 26 – Sam Kydd, Irish-born English actor (b. 1915)
- March 27 – Harriet Adams, American novelist (b. 1892)
- March 28 – William Giauque, Canadian chemist, Nobel Prize laureate (b. 1895)
- March 29 – Carl Orff, German composer (b. 1895)

April

Ville Ritola

- April 3 – Warren Oates, American actor (b. 1928)
- April 5 – Abe Fortas, U.S. Supreme Court Justice (b. 1910)
- April 9 – Robert Havemann, chemist and East German dissident (b. 1910)
- April 12 – Lenny Baker, American actor (b. 1945)
- April 15 – Arthur Lowe, British actor (b. 1915)
- April 20 – Archibald MacLeish, American poet (b. 1892)
- April 24 – Ville Ritola, Finnish athlete (b. 1896)
- April 25 – Celia Johnson, British actress (b. 1908)
- April 27 – Tom Tully, American actor (b. 1908)
- April 30 – Lester Bangs, American music journalist (b. 1948)

May

Romy Schneider

- May 1 – William Primrose, Scottish violist (b. 1903)
- May 2
  - Helmut Dantine, Austrian actor (b. 1917)
  - Hugh Marlowe, American actor (b. 1911)
- May 8 – Gilles Villeneuve, Canadian race car driver (racing accident) (b. 1950)
- May 10 – Peter Weiss, German writer and artist (b. 1916)
- May 14 – Hugh Beaumont, American actor (b. 1909)
- May 15 – Gordon Smiley, American race car driver (racing accident) (b. 1946)
- May 22 – Cevdet Sunay, ex president of Turkey (b. 1899)

- May 28 – Lt Col H. Jones, VC, British soldier (Falklands War) (b. 1940)
- May 29 – Romy Schneider, Austrian actress (b. 1938)
- May 30 – Albert Norden, German politician (b. 1904)

June

Curd Jürgens

- June 2 – Fazal Ilahi Chaudhry, President of Pakistan (b. 1904)
- June 6 – Kenneth Rexroth, American poet (b. 1905)
- June 8 – Satchel Paige, American Negro Leagues baseball player and a member of the MLB Hall of Fame (b. 1906)
- June 9 – Mirza Nasir Ahmad, 3rd Caliph of Ahmadiyya Muslim Community in Islam (b. 1909)
- June 10 – Rainer Werner Fassbinder, German film director, screenwriter and actor (b. 1945)
- June 12
  - Karl von Frisch, Austrian zoologist, recipient of the Nobel Prize in Physiology or Medicine (b. 1886)
  - Sgt Ian McKay, VC, British soldier (Falklands War) (b. 1953)
- June 13 – Riccardo Paletti, Italian Formula 1 driver (b. 1958)
- June 14 – Arthur Coles, Australian businessman and philanthropist (b. 1892)
- June 17 – Roberto Calvi, Italian banker (b. 1920)
- June 18
  - John Cheever, American novelist and short story writer (b. 1912)

- o Curd Jürgens, German actor (b. 1915)
- June 25 – Edward Hamm, American Olympic athlete (b. 1906)
- June 29 – Henry King, American film director (b. 1886)

July

Charles Robberts Swart

- July 1 – Jacobo Palm, Curaçao born composer (b. 1887)
- July 2 – Siegfried Westphal, German general (b. 1902)
- July 4
  - o Terry Higgins, early British casualty of AIDS (b. 1945)
  - o Antonio Guzmán Fernández, Dominican businessman; President of the Dominican Republic from 1978 to 1982 (b. 1911)
- July 6 – Alma Reville, English screenwriter (b. 1899)
- July 7 – Bon Maharaja, Indian guru and religious writer (b. 1901)
- July 8
  - o Isa Miranda, Italian actress (b. 1905)
  - o Albert White, American Olympic diver (b. 1895)
- July 11 – Susan Littler, British actress (b. 1948)
- July 12 – Kenneth More, English actor (b. 1914)
- July 13 – Barbara Allen Rainey, American aviator, first female pilot in the U.S. armed forces (b. 1948)
- July 16
  - o Charles Robberts Swart, 1st State President of South Africa (b. 1894)
  - o Patrick Dewaere, French actor (b. 1947)

- July 19 – John Harvey, stage and film actor (b. 1911)
- July 21 – Dave Garroway, American television host (b. 1913)
- July 22 – Lloyd Waner, American baseball player (Pittsburgh Pirates) and a member of the MLB Hall of Fame (b. 1906)
- July 23 – Vic Morrow, American actor (b. 1929)
- July 28
  - Keith Green, American gospel singer-songwriter and pianist (b. 1953)
  - Vladimir Smirnov, Soviet fencer (b. 1954)
- July 29 – Vladimir Zworykin, Russian-born inventor (b. 1889)

August

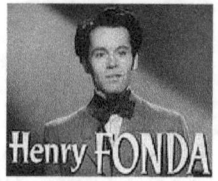

Henry Fonda

Ingrid Bergman

- August 1 – T. Thirunavukarasu, Sri Lankan Tamil politician (b. 1933)
- August 2 – Cathleen Nesbitt, British actress (b. 1888)
- August 6 – S. K. Pottekkatt, Indian writer (b. 1913)
- August 11 – Tom Drake, American actor (b. 1918)

- August 12 – Henry Fonda, American actor (b. 1905)
- August 12 – Salvador Sánchez, Mexican boxer (b. 1959)
- August 13 – Charles Walters, American film director (b. 1911)
- August 14 – Patrick Magee, Northern Irish actor (b. 1922)
- August 15 – Hugo Theorell, Swedish scientist, recipient of the Nobel Prize in Physiology or Medicine (b. 1903)
- August 18
  - Beverly Bayne, American actress (b. 1894)
  - Vladek Spiegelman, father of cartoonist Art Spiegelman and main character/narrator of *Maus* (a graphic novel of his life during the Holocaust) (b. 1906)
- August 20 – Ulla Jacobsson, Swedish actress (b. 1929)
- August 21 – King Sobhuza II of Swaziland, at the time the longest reigning living monarch (b. 1899)
- August 23
  - Alberto Cavalcanti, Brazilian film director (b. 1897)
  - Stanford Moore, American biochemist, Nobel Prize laureate (b. 1913)
- August 29 – Ingrid Bergman, Swedish actress (b. 1915)

September

Grace Kelly

- September 2
  - Tom Baker, American actor (b. 1940)
  - Jay Novello, American actor (b. 1904)

- September 5 – Douglas Bader, British fighter pilot and inspirational leader during the Battle of Britain (b. 1910)
- September 11 – Wifredo Lam, Cuban artist (b. 1902)
- September 14
  - Bachir Gemayel, President-elect of Lebanon (b. 1947)
  - Grace Kelly, American actress; Princess of Monaco (b. 1929)
- September 16 – Rolfe Sedan, American actor (b. 1896)
- September 17 – Ettore DeGrazia, American artist (b. 1909)
- September 21 – Hovhannes Bagramyan, Soviet Armenian military commander and Marshal of the Soviet Union (b. 1897)
- September 23 – Jimmy Wakely, American Country-Western singer and actor (b. 1914)
- September 28 – Mabel Albertson, American actress (b. 1901)
- September 30 – Bill George, American football player (Chicago Bears); member of the Pro Football Hall of Fame (b. 1929)

October

- October 3 – Vivien Merchant, British actress (b. 1929)
- October 4
  - Criswell, American psychic, entertainer (b. 1907)
  - Glenn Gould, Canadian pianist (b. 1932)
  - Leroy Grumman, American aeronautical engineer, test pilot, and industrialist. (b. 1895)
- October 8
  - Philip Noel-Baker, Baron Noel-Baker, Canadian-born peace activist; recipient of the Nobel Peace Prize (b. 1889)
  - Fernando Lamas, Argentine-born actor (b. 1915)
- October 9
  - Anna Freud, Austrian psychoanalyst (b. 1895)
  - Herbert Meinhard Mühlpfordt, German historian (b. 1893)
- October 10 – Jean Effel, French painter and journalist (b. 1908)
- October 16 – Hans Selye, Canadian endocrinologist (b. 1907)
- October 18
  - Bess Truman, First Lady of the United States (b. 1885)
  - Dwain Esper, director (b. 1892)

- o Pierre Mendès France, Prime Minister of France (b. 1907)
- October 20 – James Edward McGrory, Scottish football player and manager (b. 1904)
- October 22 – Savitri Devi, French-born writer and philosopher (b. 1905)
- October 25 – Arvid Wallman, Swedish diver (b. 1901)
- October 30 – Iryna Vilde, Ukrainian writer (b. 1907)
- October 31 – Dick Merrill, American aviation pioneer (b. 1894)

November

Leonid Brezhnev

Lee Patrick

- November 1
  - o James Broderick, American actor (b. 1927)
  - o King Vidor, American film director (b. 1894)
- November 4 – Dominique Dunne, American actress (b. 1959)

- November 5 – Jacques Tati, French filmmaker (b. 1907)
- November 10 – Leonid Brezhnev, Leader of the Soviet Union (b. 1906)
- November 11 – S. A. Ashokan, Tamil actor
- November 12 – Dorothy Round Little, English tennis champion (b. 1908)
- November 12 – Patrick Cowley, American disco and Hi-NRG dance music composer and recording artist (b. 1950)
- November 15
  - Vinoba Bhave, Indian educator (b. 1895)
  - Dick Randall, Australian public servant (b. 1906)
- November 17
  - Ruth Donnelly, American actress (b. 1896)
  - Duk Koo Kim, South Korean boxer (b. 1955)
  - Eduard Tubin, Estonian composer (b. 1905)
- November 21 – Lee Patrick, American actress (b. 1901)
- November 22 – Jean Batten, New Zealand aviator (b. 1909)
- November 23
  - Benny Friedman, American football player (Brooklyn Dodgers) and a member of the Pro Football Hall of Fame (b. 1905)
  - Grady Nutt, American humorist (b. 1934)
- November 24 – Barack Obama, Sr., father of US President Barack Obama (b. 1936)
- November 25 – Hugh Harman, cartoon animator (b. 1903)
- November 26 – Juhan Aavik, Estonian composer (b. 1884)
- November 29 – Percy Williams, Canadian athlete (b. 1908)

December

Arthur Rubinstein

Jack Webb

- December 2 – Marty Feldman, British comedian and writer (b. 1934)
- December 7 – Will Lee, American actor who played Mr. Hooper on *Sesame Street* (b. 1908)
- December 8 – Marty Robbins, American singer (b. 1925)
- December 10 – Freeman Fisher Gosden, American actor (b. 1899)
- December 16 – Colin Chapman, British designer, inventor, and builder in the automotive industry (b. 1928)
- December 17 – Homer S. Ferguson, American politician (b. 1889)
- December 18 – Hans-Ulrich Rudel, German World War II dive bomber pilot (b. 1916)
- December 20 – Arthur Rubinstein, Polish-born pianist and conductor (b. 1887)
- December 21 – Charles Hapgood, American college professor (b. 1904)
- December 23 – Jack Webb, American actor (b. 1920)
- December 24 – Louis Aragon, French writer (b. 1897)

- December 27 – John Swigert, American astronaut (b. 1931)
- December 29 – Hermann Balck, German general (b. 1893)

Nobel Prizes

- Physics – Kenneth G. Wilson
- Chemistry – Aaron Klug
- Medicine – Sune K. Bergström, Bengt I. Samuelsson, John R. Vane
- Literature – Gabriel García Márquez
- Peace – Alva Myrdal, Alfonso García Robles
- Economics – George Stigler

In the News

Wave of Terrorist attacks in France by Carlos the Jackal.

Argentina invades the Falkland Islands / Maldives on March 19th , and the UK sends the Royal Navy, RAF and the Army and retakes possession of the Falkland Islands during the conflict the Nuclear submarine HMS Conqueror sinks the Argentine cruiser General Belgrano. Argentina surrenders on June 14th.

Israeli forces invade Lebanon.

The largest cash robbery in History occurs in New York when $9,800,000 is stolen from an armored car.

Disney Futuristic Park EPCOT (Experimental Community Of Tomorrow)is opened.

Michael Fagan Brakes Into The Queens Bedroom in Buckingham Palace.

The Mary Rose, flagship of Henry VIII of England is raised in the Solent on October 11th and taken to Portsmouth Dockyard where it is preserved and on show to the public.

Channel 4 is launched in UK.

Italy Wins 1982 World Cup in Spain.

First CD player sold in Japan.

Graceland the home of Elvis Presley opens to the public.

Popular Films - E.T. the Extra-Terrestrial, Rocky III, On Golden Pond, Porky's, An Officer and a Gentleman.

1982 Calendar

January 1982

Sun	Mon	Tue	Wed	Thu	Fri	Sat
					1	2
3	4	5	6	7	8	9
10	11	12	13	14	15	16
17	18	19	20	21	22	23
24	25	26	27	28	29	30
31						

February 1982

Sun	Mon	Tue	Wed	Thu	Fri	Sat
	1	2	3	4	5	6
7	8	9	10	11	12	13
14	15	16	17	18	19	20
21	22	23	24	25	26	27
28						

March 1982

Sun	Mon	Tue	Wed	Thu	Fri	Sat
	1	2	3	4	5	6
7	8	9	10	11	12	13
14	15	16	17	18	19	20
21	22	23	24	25	26	27
28	29	30	31			

April 1982

Sun	Mon	Tue	Wed	Thu	Fri	Sat
				1	2	3
4	5	6	7	8	9	10
11	12	13	14	15	16	17
18	19	20	21	22	23	24
25	26	27	28	29	30	

May 1982

Sun	Mon	Tue	Wed	Thu	Fri	Sat
						1
2	3	4	5	6	7	8
9	10	11	12	13	14	15
16	17	18	19	20	21	22
23	24	25	26	27	28	29
30	31					

June 1982

Sun	Mon	Tue	Wed	Thu	Fri	Sat
		1	2	3	4	5
6	7	8	9	10	11	12
13	14	15	16	17	18	19
20	21	22	23	24	25	26
27	28	29	30			

July 1982

Sun	Mon	Tue	Wed	Thu	Fri	Sat
				1	2	3
4	5	6	7	8	9	10
11	12	13	14	15	16	17
18	19	20	21	22	23	24
25	26	27	28	29	30	31

August 1982

Sun	Mon	Tue	Wed	Thu	Fri	Sat
1	2	3	4	5	6	7
8	9	10	11	12	13	14
15	16	17	18	19	20	21
22	23	24	25	26	27	28
29	30	31				

September 1982

Sun	Mon	Tue	Wed	Thu	Fri	Sat
			1	2	3	4
5	6	7	8	9	10	11
12	13	14	15	16	17	18
19	20	21	22	23	24	25
26	27	28	29	30		

October 1982

Sun	Mon	Tue	Wed	Thu	Fri	Sat
					1	2
3	4	5	6	7	8	9
10	11	12	13	14	15	16
17	18	19	20	21	22	23
24	25	26	27	28	29	30
31						

November 1982

Sun	Mon	Tue	Wed	Thu	Fri	Sat
	1	2	3	4	5	6
7	8	9	10	11	12	13
14	15	16	17	18	19	20
21	22	23	24	25	26	27
28	29	30				

December 1982

Sun	Mon	Tue	Wed	Thu	Fri	Sat
			1	2	3	4
5	6	7	8	9	10	11
12	13	14	15	16	17	18
19	20	21	22	23	24	25
26	27	28	29	30	31	

www.ingramcontent.com/pod-product-compliance
Lightning Source LLC
Chambersburg PA
CBHW060219290526
45789CB00003B/1334